I KNEW THE BRIDE

HUGO WILLIAMS

I Knew the Bride

FABER & FABER

First published in 2014
by Faber & Faber Ltd
Bloomsbury House,
74–77 Great Russell Street,
London WC1B 3DA

Typeset by RefineCatch Limited, Bungay, Suffolk
Printed in England by Martins the Printers

A CIP record for this book
is available from the British Library

ISBN 978-0-571-30888-0

2 4 6 8 10 9 7 5 3

Acknowledgements

To the editors of *London Magazine*, *London Review of Books*, *PN Review*, *Poetry Review* and *Times Literary Supplement*.

'A Boy Call' is part of a longer poem commissioned by Arts Council England to mark the bicentenary of the Abolition of the Slave Trade Act. 'Looking for a place to lie down' in 'One Summer' was inspired by a line of Elizabeth Bishop's. Manolis Savidis translated C. P. Cavafy's prose poem 'Garments'.

I would like to thank Matthew Hollis, Neil Rennie and William Wooten for help with the book, my brother Simon for some of the memories in 'I Knew the Bride' and Nick Lowe for having written the song.

Contents

I KNEW THE BRIDE

New Year Poem

The day is difficult to start.
I leave it at the top of a hill
the night before. Next morning
I release the handbrake
and the whole rickety contraption
chokes itself back to life.
I come to a stop about here.

I leave the room for a moment
and when I come back it is evening,
everything bleached and friable
in the room's diminished oxygen.
Books lie about the place
like a game of Pelmanism.
I turn them over, looking for a pair.

Sleep is the great hobby,
with footnotes on the subject of desire.
My eyes look over my shoulder,
avoiding my gaze. Is it too late
to do something useful with my life?
I feel obliged to side with myself
to make it all more fair.

The Work

The hardest part was piercing the bony wall
of the skull, just above my right ear.
Once that was done, the drill passed
easily enough through the grey matter
until it hit bone again. The satisfaction
of seeing the tip of the drill
reappearing at last, flinging off
bits of blood and bone, more than made up
for the discomfort of the procedure.

How many people can say they have
penetrated the inner space of their being
and come out on the other side?
I raised my arms in the bathroom mirror,
as if to acknowledge the applause.
I was wondering what to do for an encore
when it occurred to me to pass a length
of picture wire through my skull
and hang myself on the wall.

Eucalyptus

I suggested a brave new form
of entertainment, one based entirely
on the emotions – hope and fear
for example, the idea being
to do whatever you want,
then describe your feelings afterwards.
My whole body tingles with excitement
because it's my turn to be 'it'.

What happens next can be dangerous.
I open my wallet twice
and look at my list of excuses.
When I've worked out what I'm going to do
I wait till it's too late,
then I leave the house, slamming the front door.
Or else I forget all that
and my body falls back on the bed.

I lie there stiffly most of the time,
watching the air moving around
in the eucalyptus trees, or the trees
moving around in the air.
Either will do to describe
the sensation of watching television,
as one day leads to another
in an endless round of pleasure.

My favourite type of creativity
is collecting eucalyptus leaves
and threading them on strings
the way we used to in Australia,
or sticking them together with glue
to make sailing ships.
I half close my eyes
and imagine them bursting into flames.

My room is full to the brim
with all manner of representations,
but the lighting's not too good.
I see the outline of something useful
bobbing about on the surface
and a look of interest passes across my face.
I rise to my toes at the top of the stairs
and my body passes before my eyes.

Soul Singer

Can you hear me singing?
I have a high clear voice
like that of Percy Sledge.
I'm a soul singer
from somewhere like Macon, Georgia.

I perform mostly
country soul numbers
in the Muscle Shoals style –
Percy's 'Out of Left Field',
'You've Got My Mind Messed Up' by James Carr.

I'm not a demonstrative singer.
I don't believe in going down on one knee
like Arthur Alexander,
or asking members of the audience
to come up on stage with me.

I stand still most of the time
and let the words do the talking.
'Sugar-plum dancing on in my mind,
every day you whip me
seems like Valentine . . .'

I might throw out an arm if the mood takes me,
or place one hand on my heart.
I might close my eyes for a moment
as I take hold of the microphone.
Can you hear me singing?

Now that I've Forgotten Brighton

Bar Italia

I linger here, remembering us
braving the weather
on the other side of the glass.
I was standing at the bar when you arrived
and you signed for me to come outside
because you wanted to smoke.
We huddled together,
drinking coffee and talking,
so near I can almost touch us.

How long were we sitting there,
shivering and smoking like that?
And what were we talking about
so eagerly and anxiously
while our cigarettes went out?
We didn't mind having to light them
over and over again,
so long as we could go on sitting there,
smoking and talking.

Hotel

Our room was a summer birdcage
swinging from a hook
on the sunny side of the street.
Someone must have hung it there one day
and forgotten to bring it in.

We weren't complaining.
There was nothing under our feet
and nothing to hold on to,
but we liked the sensation
of swaying to and fro in the breeze.

Rhyming

I lie in wait for you
on the blank sheet of the bed
while you drift about the room
improvising on a theme.

You throw ideas in the air
or kick them into a corner.
You splash the walls
with the black ink of your hair.

I agree with everything you say
when you trample a wisp
of cotton underfoot
and look at me like that.

Dry Martinis

Your keyring purse
of a watermelon slice
sits smiling on my desk,

reminding me
how quick you were on the draw
when a bill came,

or a taxi took us
to the American Bar at The Savoy
for dry Martinis.

You must have slipped a smile
to the maître d'
to let me in wearing trainers.

I saw your bare arms
when you took off your coat
and let it fall behind your chair.

Falling

It isn't so much what
obstacles we encounter on the way down

as how we come to a stop
that determines our ultimate condition.

We're OK, as it were,
so long as we keep falling.

Back and Forth

I can only look on, while my hand
dials a number it knows by heart
and a bleating noise starts up
on the other side of town.

How stupid it sounds
with its ritual 'Save me, save me'
groping around in the dark.
I will her hand not to pick up.

She is sitting in the middle of her floor,
rocking back and forth to herself,
reaching for the phone,
not answering it.

Tempera

It should have been all right
to think of her breaking eggs
for experiments with tempera,
getting her fingers dirty,
getting it in her hair.

It should have been okay
to remember her skipping
for no particular reason
when she walked beside me in the street.
It should have been okay,
but it turned out not to be.

Now that I've watered the rubbish
and put the flowers out,
there is nothing left to be done
but to stop in my tracks
and look in the palm of my hand.

Love Poem

I suppose you're right and breaking up
would be quite a good thing,
but staying together
would be an equally good thing,
so whatever we decide to do
it will be all right. On balance,
I lean towards doing nothing,
but whatever happens we'll go on
seeing each other, won't we?

I suppose it wouldn't be so bad,
seeing other people for a change,
we might even find someone
we could bear to be with
for more than half an hour,
although I doubt it somehow.
Experience suggests we go on
feeling the same about everything
no matter what happens. I do anyway.

One Summer

Two hot days and nights,
then a thunderstorm after you've gone.
I count the miles
between the lightning flash
and the first rumblings
as the storm sets off northwards,
looking for a place to lie down.

Car alarms moan in the distance.
A curtain of rain hangs in the garden,
then blows indoors.
I run upstairs to check the window
and there it is –
the one in the bathroom still open
from when you were here.

Early Morning

Perhaps if I lie still
watching the tops of trees
scratching low clouds
I won't remember
her bedside manner,
her sense of etiquette.

If I let that branch
sweep the storm
into a corner of the sky
I might forget
the satisfaction she takes
in getting it just right.

If I watch that crow
flicking scrawls of black ink
from the edges of its wings
I might not remember
her saying certain things,
her throwing out one arm.

In a difficult dream
I was allowed to touch her hair.

Fate Song

A tin of salmon
a flash of lightning
everything in the world
brings her back to me
with a knock on the door
and a rain-soaked figure
who isn't really there.

A ring round the moon
the voice of Robert Johnson
nothing in the world
can forget her
and nothing ever will
except herself of course
if she were available.

So Long

Now that I've forgotten Brighton,
now that I can't remember
The King's Palace Hotel,
its pool hall and brothel,
Volk's Electric Railway
rattling over the shingle
on its way to Black Rock,
or the spray that flew in our faces
when we pulled the canvas up to our chins
for the ride on the speedboat,

now that I've forgotten
Ali Baba's Forty Thieves
poking their heads out of urns
in the window of Louis Tussaud's,
Joe Hunter's Lonely Pilgrims
playing 'The Man I Love'
in the Pavilion Gardens, I'm confident
nothing remains of that weekend
save this old theatre-club programme,
so long it has to be folded.

Actaeon

I thought of all my girlfriends
gathered together on a stage,
each of them holding up her year
and smiling attractively.
I lifted one corner of the curtain
and there they all were,
but shy and resentful now,
covering themselves from my sight.

'I didn't know you girls all
knew one another', I said,
seeing only a tumble of looks and limbs.
'What are you doing here?'
They answered that they might as well
ask me the same question.
What was the matter?
Couldn't I make up my mind?

If I had stood my ground
and said nothing, or claimed
to be just passing through,
I might have escaped their mockery,
I might have been forgiven.
Alas, I fled the scene,
dogged by indecision and regret,
torn apart by little pointed teeth.

Twenty Yards Behind

for Wilko Johnson

All those things men find so intense,
watching her walking from twenty yards behind,
women take as the most tender nonsense.

Their appreciation isn't a pretence,
but they couldn't care less what kind
of strange things we find so intense,

so long as we enjoy the performance
and what we place in their hand
isn't just some tender nonsense.

If we knew their true response,
as they threw their limbs around,
to all the things we find so intense,

we might experience detumescence,
but at least we would understand
why they talked such tender nonsense.

With a greater degree of correspondence
we might not like what we found.
All those things men find so intense
women take as the most tender nonsense.

Maquette

An introductory section, built
like the page of a history book,
bound with a spiral staircase,
descending twenty metres
in as many years,
narrowing and darkening
as it enters the tormented period
of the 1930s – recession,
suicides, musicals, a silent
mock-up of a nightclub.

A wartime section with sandbags,
gas masks, love letters, lipstick,
an air-raid shelter
with corrugated iron roof,
blackouts, searchlights, adultery,
the King and Queen to the rescue:
blood, sweat and Bovril.
We exit through a luminous arch
set in a mushroom cloud.

A backward-looking post-war section
with everything just as it was
for a moment – crinkle-cut
black and white photos
of picnics on the beach at Dymchurch,
children riding bikes,
while behind their backs
the criss-cross scaffolding poles
of wartime defences
give a nostalgic look to 1947.

An American section is in preparation.

I Knew the Bride

for my sister Polly 1950–2004

You had to go to bed ahead of us
even then, while your two older brothers
grabbed another hour downstairs.
The seven-year gap
was like a generation between us.
You played the princess,
swanning about the house
in your tablecloth wedding dress,
till we told you your knickers were dirty
and you ran upstairs to change.
Your hair was tied up
in plaits on top of your head,
showing the parting down the back
as you marched out of the room.

It wouldn't be long
till we were asking you to dance,
practising our jiving
for the Feather's Club Ball at the Lyceum.
Nobody knew so well
how to judge the turns
with perfectly tensed arms,
your ponytail flying back and forth
to 'Party Doll' by Buddy Knox.
For my speech on your wedding day
all I had to do
was read out the words
to Nick Lowe's 'I Knew the Bride
When She Used to Rock 'n' Roll'.

You used to do the pony,
you used to do the stroll,
but the bride in her wedding dress
spinning round on top of the cake,
wound down to a sense of loss
when your coach didn't come
and questions of identity
rained on your party.
The bride turned out
to be less a princess
than a walk-on part
as a lady-in-waiting
in a film of Cinderella,
The Slipper and the Rose.

A life of go-sees and
castings, followed by
the odd screen test, gave way
to a different sort of test,
with shadows for faces.
When you first crossed over
into that wintry place
you said you had a feeling even then.
The different parts of you
turned against one another,
as if they could hear you thinking.
'What you don't realise', you said,
in your new winter bonnet,
'is that hair goes with everything.'

You put yourself together
for occasional family lunches
at the Brompton Brasserie,
appearing coiffed and chic
and on time, so that I imagined you
going about all day looking like that
and even assumed you were getting better.
You fought a five-year war
with that foul thing
which deals in hope and fear,
two against one,
like the two brothers who tormented you.
It wouldn't be long
till you had to go to bed.

You turned your back on us
to protect us from your face.
You lay on the rack of yourself,
murdered by your skeleton.
Somewhere towards the end
you climbed its rickety ladder
to your full height
and stood before us one last time.
You had ordered a white stetson
from a Country music catalogue.
Perched on your coffin, it sailed
ahead of you into the flames.
I saw the parting down the back of your head
as you marched out of the room.

My Sister's Records

It isn't much to show
for a lifetime's shopping –
a few classic albums
come down to me in a cardboard box.

I feel sorry for them,
standing alone on their shelves,
filed under their different categories.
I should have let them stay together,
so they could talk to one another.

A sense of her sweeps in
every time I put on Al Green's
'You Ought to Be with Me',
or 'Call Me, Come Back Home'.

The Fifties

Remember porters? Weatherbeaten old boys
with watery blue eyes, who found you a corner seat
'facing the engine' and stowed your luggage
in a net above your head? You gave them a coin,
worth almost nothing, even then.
They touched their caps and thanked you,
as they struggled out through the sliding doors
of the compartment, into the corridor.
You used to worry vaguely
that they wouldn't have time to get down.

A Boy Call

The long cry of 'BOY . . .', falsetto,
travels down two flights
and bursts like a blow to the head
through the last door on the left,
where I am struggling with my essay
on the American Civil War.
My room is furthest away
from the Common Room. Only Barnes
is behind me in the scrum
of tailcoats and bumfreezers
jockeying for position in the corridor.
He takes hold of my tails
and whips me against the wall.

Church is standing on the stairs,
looking down at me. He's wearing
the dark blue waistcoat
with silver stars, a clove carnation,
braided tailcoat and sponge bag trousers.
He scribbles a note, twists it
into the customary knot
and chucks it down to me.
'Take this to Howe in Chamiers.'
As soon as I am out of sight
I unfold the note and read,
'What do you think of this one?
Get him to do the Charleston.'

Brow

The brow of the hill rose steeply ahead of me,
a patch of light like a window
in its polished surface.

I would set my foot on that slick of black ice.
Its luminous white line would lead me
over the horizon of my father's head.

I Was Like

Stairs are the sort of place
where unnatural tenses
produce the effect
of treading water.
It can be creative
in a dumb sort of way,
floating around
on up-draughts of warm air,
or it can be annoying
when you come to a stop
and all your possessions
go hurtling past you
down the waste-chute.

When I hear the knock
I'm like 'This is it'.
The end of the world!
Now everything depends
on my ability
to surf the crest
of a monstrous billow,
to dabble my toes
in the debris and dust
of the perfect provisional
without the embarrassment
of killing myself
playing 'air bannisters'.

Every so often
my head appears like a buoy

out of the domestic fog.
My heartbeat quickens
to a thrilling drum roll
announcing my arrival.
If the house were removed
I would be seen
bouncing up and down
in my bouncy castle.
I put a cross on the wall
to mark where I am
before I have to fall back.

The light in the hall
is my guilty secret.
It clicks on automatically
as I come downstairs.
The orange stair carpet
never seems to be happy
till its forward edge
is sticking out into the street.
Every day I pull it back,
taking hold of one end
and shaking it out
like shaking out
ripples of orange mud.

The Chinese Stock Exchange

The teenage con-girl in martial arts gear
hooks me like a numbered fish out of the night
and holds me up to the light like a ten pound note.
She lets me go ahead of her up some stairs,
through a door marked 'Chinese Stock Exchange'.
'You pay me now I come back later', she explains.

I sit down with the other hopefuls in front of
a big old TV set with the sound turned down.
Karl Malden's nose pokes suspiciously into our lives
from some long ago *Streets of San Francisco*.
'Will she be long?' I ask a man in pyjamas.
'Not long', he replies. 'Tonight very busy night'.

The Bar in the Wood

Ripped from its moorings in some
remote village pub,
the old bar rots drunkenly here
at the party of the seasons.

Leaves come up over the footrail.
Circles of mould
crowd the blistered counter-top
where orange slugs crawl.

That must be me over there,
leaning on the old bar,
trying to call home,
saying I'm going to be late.

Coming Back

The old upright shopping bicycle
has the wrong saddle, a racing one,
more like an iron bar than a saddle.

I perch on one side or the other,
carrier-bags swinging from the handlebars
full of provisions for the weekend.

It's hard work pedalling uphill in the rain,
but after a while I don't seem to mind.
Nothing seems to matter any more.

As if from long custom, I hand over
the groceries at the kitchen window,
take off my shoes and go upstairs to change.

As I draw the bedroom curtains I see you
hurrying down the path with an umbrella
on your way to fetch a salad for dinner.

Upside Down

Cups and saucers, glasses,
bowls, anything remotely
concave, she turns upside down,
leaving a suction mark on the table,
a taste of soap
round the rim of a tooth mug.
Even the triangular container
for cutlery gets up-ended
for no particular reason.
I nearly mentioned it once,
but managed to hold my tongue.
I would be sorry never again
to see things upside down.

Something More Serious

I was feeling around in the water,
looking for my favourite mug,
when I imagined a chopping-up knife
going in under a fingernail,
a broken wine glass slitting my wrist.

It's usually all right of course,
providing you're careful –
except for that one time, remember,
when a slight pain in the finger
heralded something more serious.

A Late Caller

Someone's banging on the front door,
trying to get in with the wrong key.
He seems to think he lives here
and is being prevented from entering
his own house. I'm a dirty rotten bastard
for changing the locks on him.

All right, I decide to let him in,
if only to prove him wrong. He calms down
a little when he sees the living room
and we stand there for a moment,
looking round us admiringly
at what I've done with the old place.

At the Pillars

i.m. Mick Imlah

Everyone was saying their favourite word.
Yours was 'suddenly'.
Other members of the herd
chose something funny or absurd,
'lackadaisical' or 'haphazard'.
We were laughing and drinking happily,
saying our favourite word.
Yours was 'suddenly'.

The Golden Conjuror's Outfit

The make-up, the wig,
everything is exactly right
for appearing in public
to the roar of time passing.
'And for my next trick . . .'
You close your eyes for a moment
and whisper 'Abracadabra!'
How brilliant to be nobody,
knowing nothing, going nowhere,
as when you asked as a child,
'Are we nearly there?'

What you're standing up in
is what you lie down in.
It comes off easily,
or they undo the back.
Your understanding of this
is a nice clean turn-down.
You smooth it with your hands.
The thing about spoons, you say,
you can't tell which way up they are!
You haven't thanked everyone
for the Golden Conjuror's Outfit?

Garments

from a prose poem by C. P. Cavafy

In an old trunk or in an ebony chest
I put away the yellow clothes of my childhood,
my favourite yellow clothes.

I put away the blue clothes I wore as a boy,
the blue clothes that boys always wear,
followed by the red clothes of my youth,

the exciting red clothes of a young man.
I put away the red clothes, then I put away
the blue clothes again, more faded this time.

I wear black clothes. I live in a black house.
Sometimes at night I open the ebony chest
and gaze with longing at my beautiful clothes.

A Twitch of the Mouth

1.

I've been acting strangely again,
ducking my head, spinning round.
I stand out of sight behind a curtain,
crying and laughing to myself.
I've been told there is something exciting
waiting for me later on,
if I promise not to make a fuss.
I wait till everyone has gone home,
then I creep downstairs and have a look around.
If nobody can see me,
does that mean I've won?

I don't like the way
I've tucked that piece of paper
over a picture frame,
as if I had something to hide.
Things obscuring me, or my obscuring them?
I wouldn't blame me for not knowing!
Since I am here, I reason,
I must be answering my own plea
for a better understanding.
I run round the room on the furniture.
I lick my finger going through a door.

I was supposed to put everything in bags
and wait on the landing,
but I didn't want to do that.
I was standing over by the window, looking out.

Parks were the sort of place
I imagined myself strutting around
in uniform. There was the lilac tree
that shed dew on my shoulder.
Perhaps I could think about that?
I thought about someone at school
whose nickname was 'Sausages'.

2.

The universe turns draughty. Doors don't fit.
I signal left for bathroom,
turn sharply right for something to eat.
I have come to a point in the day
when it tips up like a see-saw
and I have to be careful.
I try a twitch of the mouth.
It's annoying when little imitation things
get inside other things,
so that when you pick them up they aren't there.
But I'd better not say that.

I was carrying it upstairs on a tray,
whatever it was,
bumping open doors with my hip,
going through backwards as instructed.
Every time I went through a door
I went through twice.
I discovered a wafer-thin silence between rooms,
where everything piled up.

I put it down a moment ago, whatever it was,
now all I can make out
is a burn-hole spreading.

What was the name of that thing the other night
that was like the name of the man
who wrote 'Stardust'?
Everyone knows what I mean
when I wave my hands in the air
explaining a joke in sign language
about crashing into a wall.
They tell me I'm moving forward
at exactly the right speed for comedy.
The man with the polystyrene coffee cup
is practically paralysed with laughter.

Patent Pending

The slightest movement of the body,
whether of genuine revival
or only a false alarm
caused by pockets of air
trapped in the abdomen,
triggers a sensitive
release mechanism
housed in a spring-loaded ball
positioned over the heart.

If this ball is disturbed
by so much as a twitching nerve-end,
a message is transmitted
to a box on the surface,
which immediately flies open,
admitting air to the coffin.
A flag rises in warning,
a bell rings for half an hour,
a lamp burns after sunset.

From the Dialysis Ward

O passenger, pray list and catch
Our sighs and piteous groans,
Half stifled in this jumbled patch
Of wrenched memorial stones!

         – THOMAS HARDY, 'The Levelled Churchyard'

If I'm Early

Every other day I follow the route
of the Midland Railway
to where it cuts through
St Pancras Old Church Cemetery.
I might go into the church
and heave a sigh or two
before continuing via a gate
set in the cemetery wall
to the Mary Rankin Wing
of St Pancras Hospital.

As a young man, Thomas Hardy
supervised the removal of bodies
from part of the cemetery
to make way for the trains.
He placed the headstones
round an ash tree sapling,
now grown tall, where I stop sometimes
to look at the stones
crowding round the old tree
like children listening to a story.

[45]

Good Thanks

They always ask how you are
when you arrive,
but they know already of course.

It's pretty obvious
from the pleading look on your face
and your dialysis tan

that you're a regular here
and it doesn't do
to say you feel terrible.

You're lucky to be alive,
but you don't see it like that.
You think you're being brave.

A joke might have done
to break the ice between you,
but you can't think of one.

You're that woebegone figure
carrying a satchel,
who isn't funny at all.

A Game of Dialysis

The home team appears
in a blue strip, while the visitors
keep on their street clothes.
We find our positions
from the file with our name on it
placed beside our bed.
Now all we can do is wait
for the opposition to make a move.
We don't like our chances.

The action commences
with the home team wandering about,
or making a tour of the circuit.
Certain moves are typical –
lengthwise, for example,
carrying something,
is a popular move, or scoring points
by passing back and forth
between the glove dispenser
and the needle disposal box.

The visitors can only look on
as the enemy's game plan emerges.
We score by keeping quiet
about our disadvantages,
or saying something funny.
Whether anyone gets hurt

depends on who is marking whom.
The blues fan out round the room.
Each of them is doing something difficult
to somebody lying down.

Grand Canyon Suite

Every few minutes someone's alarm goes off
because of a blood clot,
or a sudden fall in pressure,
then the first two notes of Ferde Grofé's
'On the Trail' goes clip-clopping
down the Grand Canyon of the ward.

It isn't long before the first two notes
are joined by the same two notes
from a neighbouring machine,
then another two, till the whole
hopeless blind herd
is clip-clopping off into the sunset.

A Healthy Interest

Nurse Anthony thinks I show potential
for taking more responsibility
with my treatment. Other patients go round
collecting requirements
from the various trolleys – bandages,
plasters, needles, spray,
paper napkins, disinfectant wipes –
and putting them in the blue tray
prior to needling. Did I know
that some patients do their own needling?

He looks disappointed with me.
My indifference is fear, he says.
I need to take more interest in my case.
I need to make a note
of my fluctuating water, weight
and blood pressure levels, only then
can I come to terms with my condition.
I'm doomed, apparently, if I persist
in cutting off home from hospital.
He's only trying to help me.

I should realise I'm an ideal candidate
for home dialysis, which only involves
minor plumbing in the bedroom
and a stent in your stomach every night.
The increased risk of infection
is practically negligible
if you follow the hygiene instructions

and don't sleepwalk (laughs).
If I'm concerned about anything
I could take a course like Mr and Mrs Vale.

Yes, but What's Your Dry Weight?

The bio-impediment weighing machine
detects the amount of water in your system
and subtracts its findings
from your overall bodyweight
to give you your 'dry weight',
the Holy Grail of dialysis.
You hear the words 'dry weight'
being held up as an example
of a better you just out of reach.
There's a constant bargaining
between you and your nurse
about how much they can 'take off'
without your passing out,
or having to be up-ended.
You agree to two litres, max,
And leave feeling awful.

The Art of Needling

You find out early on
that some of the nurses
are better than others
at the art of needling.
You have to ascertain

who's on duty today
that knows what they're doing,
someone familiar
with your fistula arm,
and beg him to 'put you on'.

If he's any good
he'll take his time
raising or lowering the bed,
laying out his things on the tray.
He won't forget the spray.

He'll listen to the 'bruit'
produced by your fistula.
He'll note the 'thrill' of it,
feel it with his finger.
Only then will he go in.

Even so, a wayward needle
can pierce a fistula wall,
causing a 'blow' to occur.
Then you have to go to A&E
for a fistulaplasty.

The Angel of the Needles

The beauty of the Indian nurse
puts the fear of God in me
when she approaches my bed
carrying the blue tray.

Did she have to take a needling test
like other mortals?
Or did they let her in
for being one of the angels?

I want her to like me,
but I have to look away
when she strips the paper from the needles
and bends over me.

She applies the tourniquet
and lays a finger on the vein.
Something about her touch
makes the needles melt in my flesh.

She takes away the pain
by telling me in a mournful tone
about her son Ibrahim
who is bullied at school
for the mixed pigments on his face.

The Dog

A dog has got hold of my arm
and is dragging me down.
Its canines pierce an artery.
Its entrails twitch with my blood.

Whenever I am brought in
for further questioning,
the dog stands over me,
grinding its teeth in my flesh.

It's like being nailed to the floor
and told to relax.
Blood spurts like a confession.

This is what dogs are for,
to find out who you are.

I watch its eyes going round,
analysing the evidence.
I'll admit to anything.

The Song of the Needles

Needles have the sudden beauty
of a first line.
They're always new and surprising
as they burst from their paper covering.
They sing as they hit the air.

You catch sight of them
out of the corner of your eye,
glinting softly to themselves
as they contemplate their next move.

What they're suggesting is inspired,
but a certain sadness
attends their description
of what is going on.
You don't know whether to look away,
or accept what they're saying.

If you're lucky you'll feel a pop
as one of them enters your fistula
and a cool feeling of recognition
spreads up through your arm.

A Recommendation

I'd have to recommend dialysis
to anyone looking for a break
in their daily routine,
anyone averse to work
and the difficulties of starting,
who derives no pleasure
from getting things done.

The beauty of dialysis
is that it saves you the trouble
of planning too far ahead,
of working out what you're going to do
with your afternoons.
It uses up half your life
without your lifting a finger.

Diality

The shock of remembering,
having forgotten for a second,
that this isn't a cure,
but a kind of false health,
like drug addiction.

It performs the trick
of sieving you clean of muck
for a day or two
by means of a transparent tube
full of pinkish sand.

Your kidneys like the idea
of not having to
work for a living
and gradually shut down.
Then you stop peeing.

Dialysis is bad for you.
It takes you by the hand,
but it doesn't lead you anywhere.
The shock of remembering,
having forgotten for a second.

A Living

Every other day it is Sunday
with Monday's sickly grin
appearing on the horizon.
Thanks for reminding me
of the bus ride with sandwiches.

When Monday comes round
for the third time that week
I go to work lying down,
I turn myself inside out,
I scrub my blood for a living.

Every other day it is Sunday,
but I don't feel like Sunday lunch.
I take everything out of the fridge,
then I eat a strawberry.

Ray's Way

Ray Blighter appears in the doorway
of the dialysis ward
in all his ruined finery –
waistcoat, buttonhole, blazer,
eyebrows dashed in with mascara –
and pauses for a moment to ensure
all eyes are upon him.

'MY NAME IS BOND,' he shouts
to the assembled company,
'JAMES FUCKING BOND.'
He sets off down the line of beds,
muttering, looking straight ahead,
yellowing grey flannels
flapping round his ankles.

He's two hours late,
having been 'run over by a bus',
but God help anyone who's taken
his precious corner bed.
If the rabbi is there ahead of him
he's liable to turn around
and go home again.

He sets out his life
on the table across his bed –
beer cans, biscuits, betting slips,
a hairbrush, aftershave,
a radio tuned to Radio 2,

the only one allowed on the ward
because Ray is a 'character'.

He goes and stands in the fire exit
for his ritual 'last cigarette'
before he kills himself.
'Do you smoke Morland Specials
with the three gold rings?' I ask.
Ray lifts a coal-black eyebrow.
'Do you think I look like Sean Connery?'

He acted with Sean, he tells me,
in several James Bond films,
including *Live and Let Die*.
'And no, not as a bleeding extra!'
When he goes on to describe his role
in Bridge on the Fucking River Kwai
the penny drops.

Trapped in his own Japanese
prisoner-of-war camp for ten years,
he's lied and cursed his way free.
'I won't be coming in on Monday',
he tells me confidentially.
'I'm going to the fucking races.'
Of course he is. I may be there myself.

The Fields Beneath

I make my tour
of the garden waiting room
where the tall trees
wander among the corpses.

I might go past
the last resting place
of Sir John Soane
in his stone telephone kiosk,

or the wooden bench
where the Beatles sat
on their 'Mad Day Out',
July 28th, 1968.

The body of J. C. Bach,
'The English Bach',
lies somewhere near here,
lost to the railway in 1865.

A plaque remembers him
as Queen Charlotte's music tutor
who collaborated with someone
and died young.

Perhaps Jerry Cruncher got him,
or perhaps he survived
and is strolling with his friend
in the fields beneath.

Zombie

I'm technically dead, they tell me,
but I remember being alive
as if it were yesterday.
I'm covered in mud, like a zombie,
swimming around
in the storms of a new grave.

I remember the world above
and what it was like up there,
thanks to a friend
who sucks my blood for me.
He keeps me alive
in the sense that memories are alive.

Going Home

Leaving behind the Gothic frowns
of the former workhouse, I pass through a gate
into a churchyard overhung by great trees,
where the nurses go to smoke.

Mary Wollstonecraft's tomb,
where Shelley proposed to her daughter,
escaped demolition by Thomas Hardy
and seems to be plunging off into a storm.

Shelley's heart, wrapped in a brown paper parcel,
Hardy took by train to Bournemouth,
sitting in a first class compartment
with the heart on his knee.

Prayer Before Sleeping

Send me a poem, God,
before I go to bed.
Let me feel its breath on my face,
its flash of straw.

Throw me a first line
that I can sleep on.
Fireflies in a Mason jar!
Let me lose myself over there.

If you've got nothing better,
sling me a wrong one
that'll make me laugh
then take off into the blue.

Slip me some sort of clue
that knows what to do with me
and I promise I'll be good.